A CURIOUS COLLECTION
OF
ANIMALS

Weird, Wonderful, and Wild

An Imprint of Sterling Publishing Co., Inc.
1166 Avenue of the Americas
New York, NY 10036

Text by Camilla de la Bedoyere and Nancy Dickmann

ISBN: 978-1-4351-6571-7

Manufactured in Guangdong, China
Lot #:
2   4   6   8   10   9   7   5   3   1
12/16

www.sterlingpublishing.com

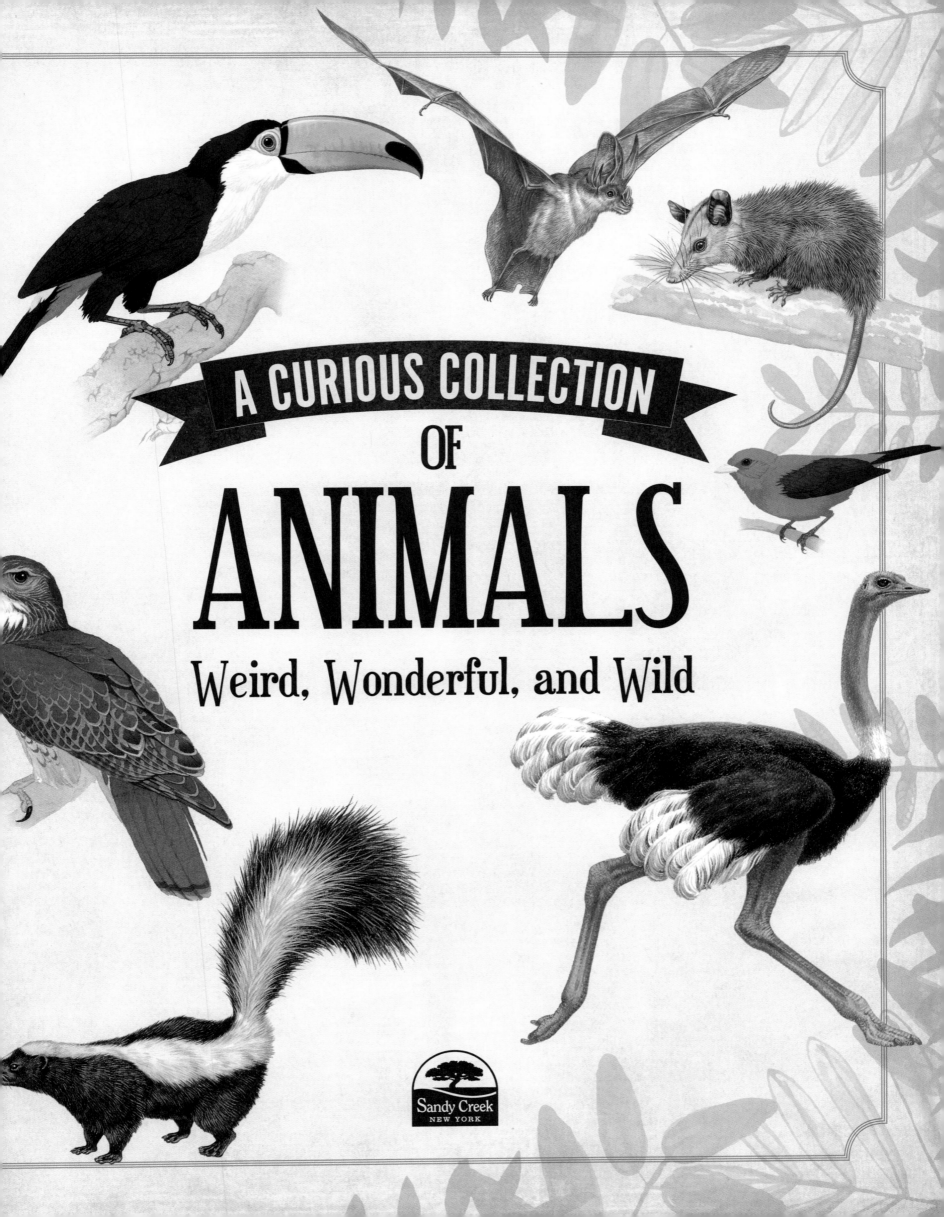

A CURIOUS COLLECTION

OF

ANIMALS

Weird, Wonderful, and Wild

Sandy Creek
NEW YORK

Introduction

The world is full of amazing animals, from tiny ants to enormous elephants. Animals live on land, in rivers, in soil, and even in the deepest parts of the ocean. They can be scaly, stripy, squishy, spotted, or scary—or sometimes a mixture of many of these! Although they are all different, they fit into six main groups.

Types of Animals

MAMMALS
Mammals breathe air and produce milk to feed their young. Most have hair or fur.

OKAPI

GOPHER SNAKE

REPTILES
Reptiles are cold-blooded creatures with scaly bodies. Most lay eggs, and many spend time both on land and in water.

WILD BOAR WITH YOUNG

DUSKY SALAMANDER

AMERICAN ALLIGATOR

WALLACE'S FLYING FROG

AMPHIBIANS
Amphibians spend part of their lives on land and part in water. They are cold-blooded and take in oxygen through their moist skin.

BIRDS

Birds have two legs, two wings, feathers, and a beak. They all lay eggs, but not all of them can fly.

CRESTED TREE SWIFT

ECLECTUS PARROT

ZANDER

WELS

FISH

Fish live in water, and they use their gills to get oxygen from it. Most have fins to help them move through the water.

INVERTEBRATES

Any animal without a backbone is an invertebrate. This group includes insects, spiders, shellfish, worms, jellyfish, and many more.

ARMORED MILLIPEDE

COMMON OCTOPUS

CLICK BEETLE

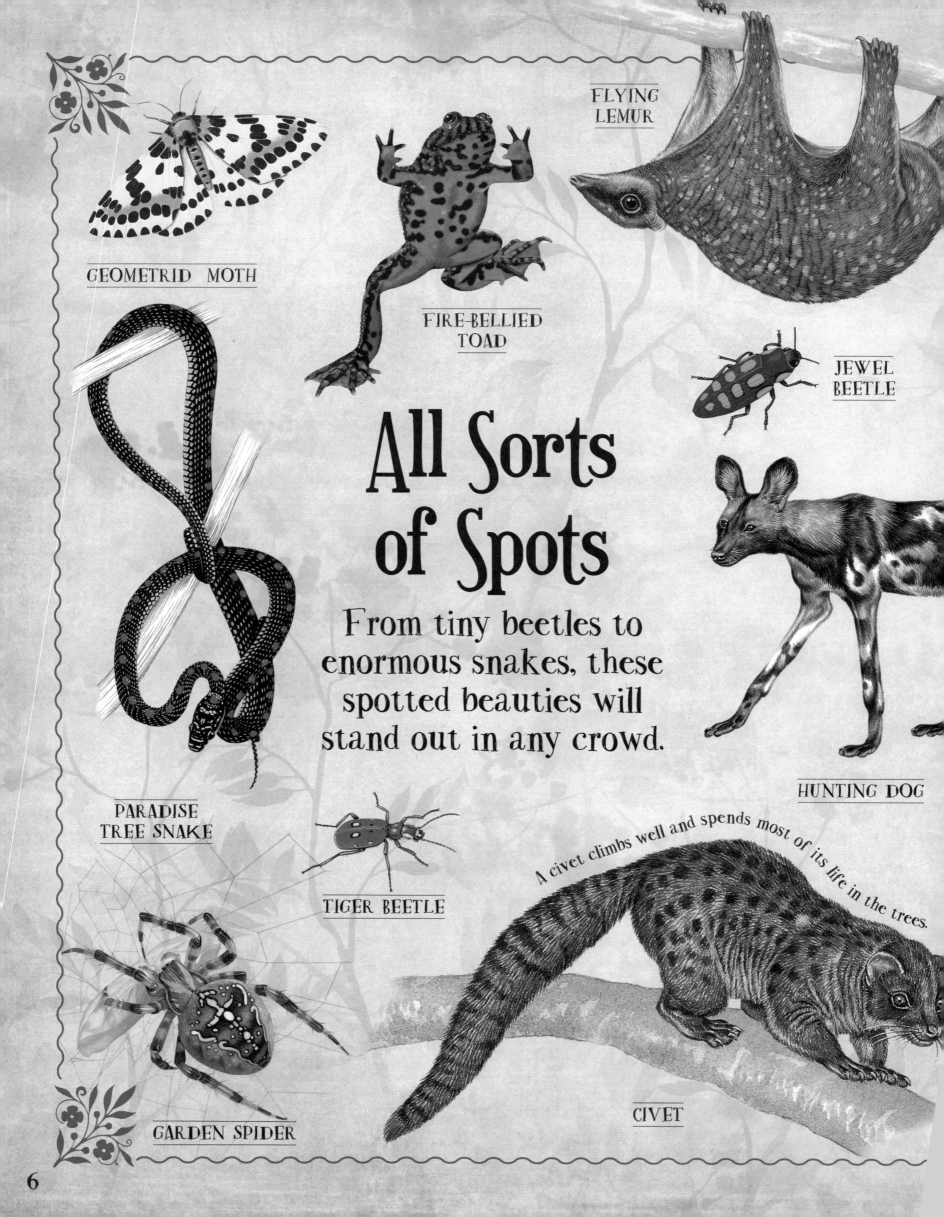

GEOMETRID MOTH

FIRE-BELLIED TOAD

FLYING LEMUR

JEWEL BEETLE

All Sorts of Spots

From tiny beetles to enormous snakes, these spotted beauties will stand out in any crowd.

PARADISE TREE SNAKE

TIGER BEETLE

HUNTING DOG

A civet climbs well and spends most of its life in the trees.

GARDEN SPIDER

CIVET

A limpkin wades through muddy swamps, using its curved beak to find snails and mussels to eat.

LIMPKIN

Only male peacocks have long trains of beautiful feathers.

PEACOCK

ANACONDA

TRAGOPAN

Leopards are excellent climbers, and they often haul the bodies of their prey up into trees so that other animals don't steal them.

LEOPARD

LADYBIRD

SNOW LEOPARD

STARLING

SALAMANDER

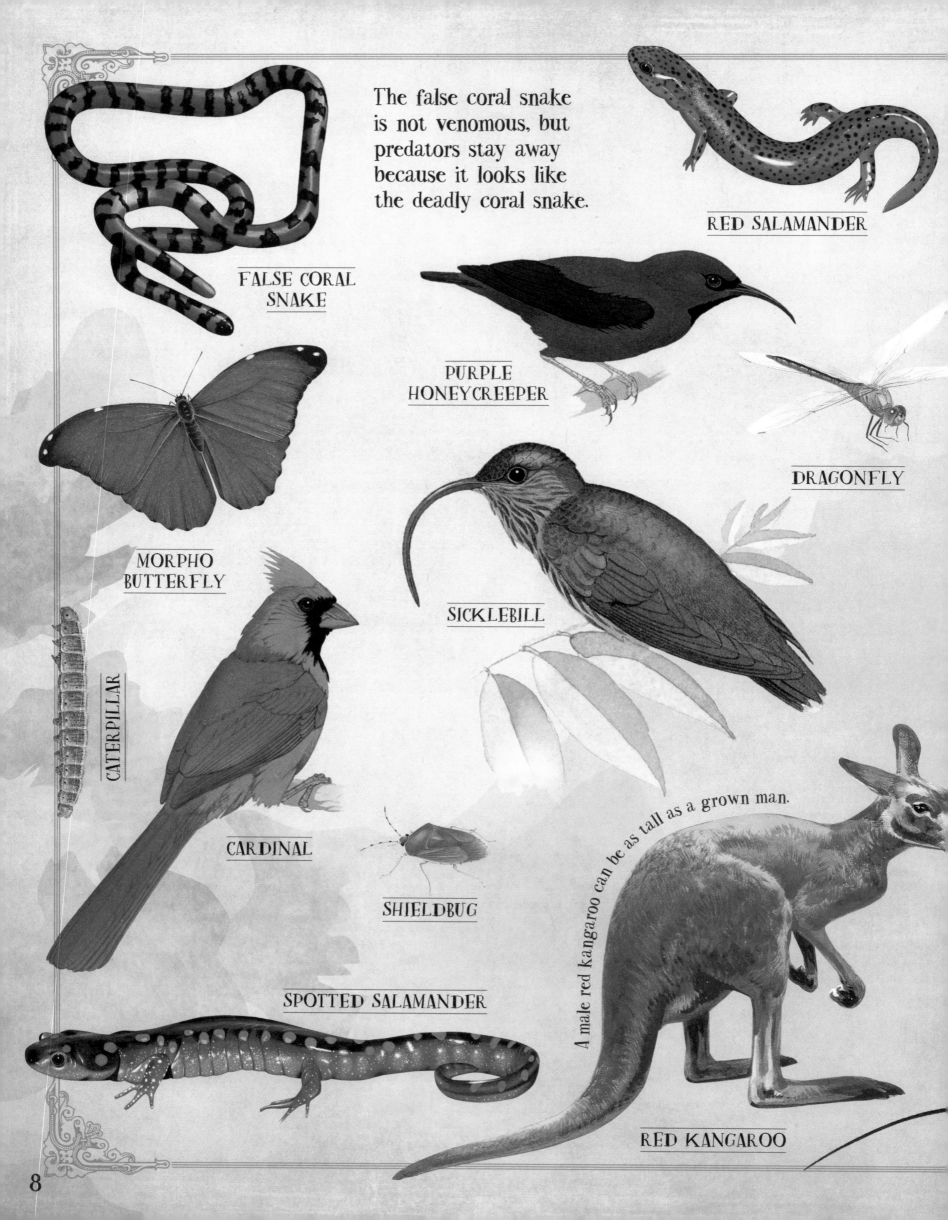

The false coral snake is not venomous, but predators stay away because it looks like the deadly coral snake.

RED SALAMANDER

FALSE CORAL SNAKE

PURPLE HONEYCREEPER

DRAGONFLY

MORPHO BUTTERFLY

SICKLEBILL

CATERPILLAR

CARDINAL

SHIELDBUG

A male red kangaroo can be as tall as a grown man.

SPOTTED SALAMANDER

RED KANGAROO

CHAMELEON

VELVET MITE

BLUE JAY

Red foxes can live in almost any habitat.

RED FOX

BUTTERFLY

LEAF INSECT

Colorful Creatures

Animal life comes in every color of the rainbow!

TIGER SALAMANDER

CAECILIAN

A male green anole lizard fans out the flap of pink skin on his throat in order to attract a female.

SCARLET TANAGER

GREEN ANOLE LIZARD

LAPWING

Sharp Eyes

The sense of sight helps an animal to find food and spot danger— and these creatures' eyes have that covered!

WESTERN TARSIER

WOLF SPIDER

BEE

JAGUAR

SNOWY OWL

Snowy owls can see well during the day and at night. They can also turn their heads almost completely around, to look in all directions.

MARSUPIAL FROG

VICUNA

Vicunas live in the Andes Mountains of South America.

LOCUST

WEB-FOOTED GECKO

HOUSEFLIES

Most animals have two eyes. Which of these creatures has more than two?

ANSWER ON PAGE 64

The "eyes" on an Indian cobra's throat are really just spots. They confuse predators who hunt the cobra.

INDIAN COBRA

AYE-AYE

11

BOLL WEEVIL

A boll weevil uses its long snout to bore into the seed pods of cotton plants.

SIDEWINDER

A Tasmanian devil's powerful jaws can crush bones.

TASMANIAN DEVIL

Which of these super scary animals is the strongest, for its size?

ANSWER ON PAGE 64

Super Scary

These animals may be small, but you wouldn't want to pick a fight with them!

ICHNEUMON WASP

A female praying mantis often eats the male she mates with.

PRAYING MANTIS

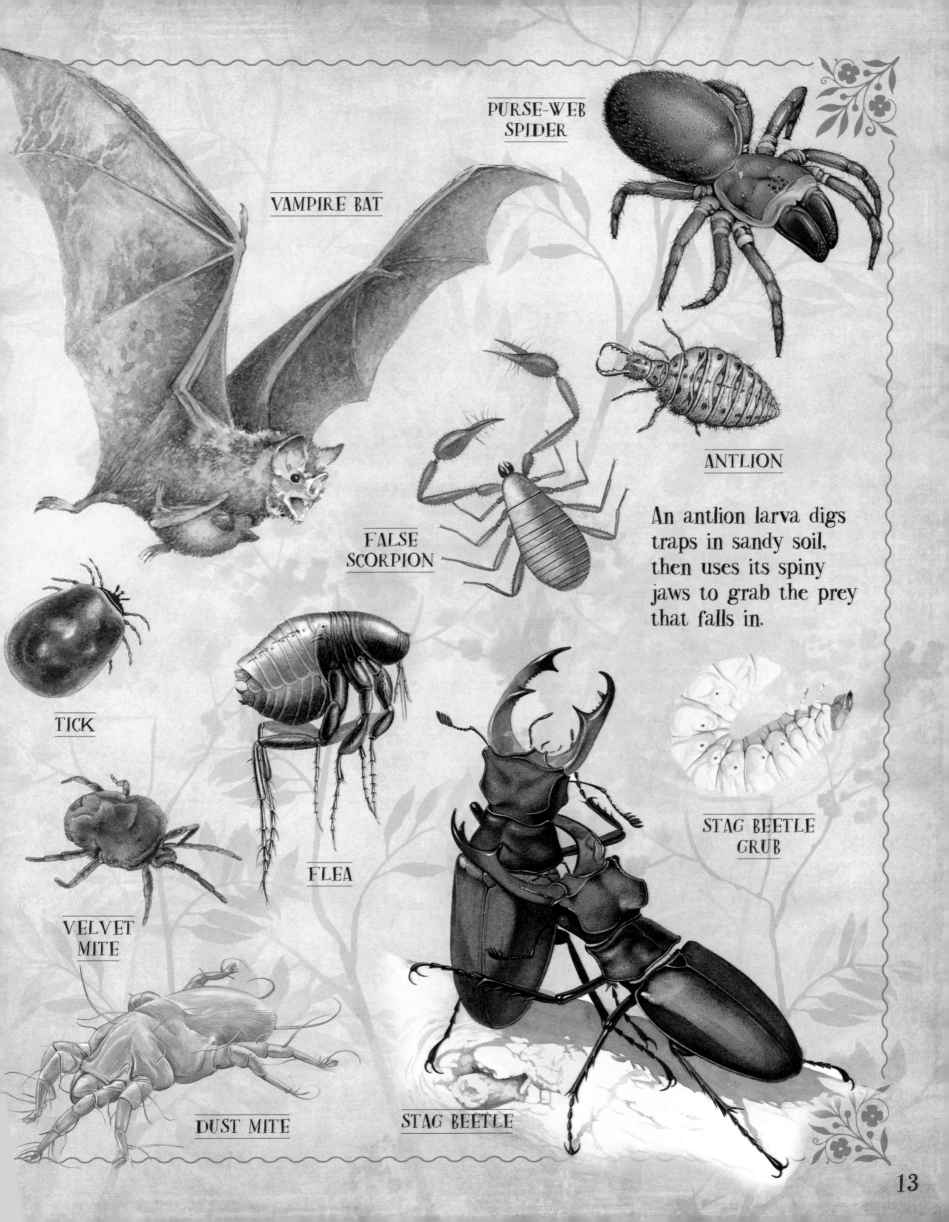

PURSE-WEB
SPIDER

VAMPIRE BAT

ANTLION

FALSE
SCORPION

An antlion larva digs
traps in sandy soil,
then uses its spiny
jaws to grab the prey
that falls in.

TICK

STAG BEETLE
GRUB

FLEA

VELVET
MITE

DUST MITE

STAG BEETLE

13

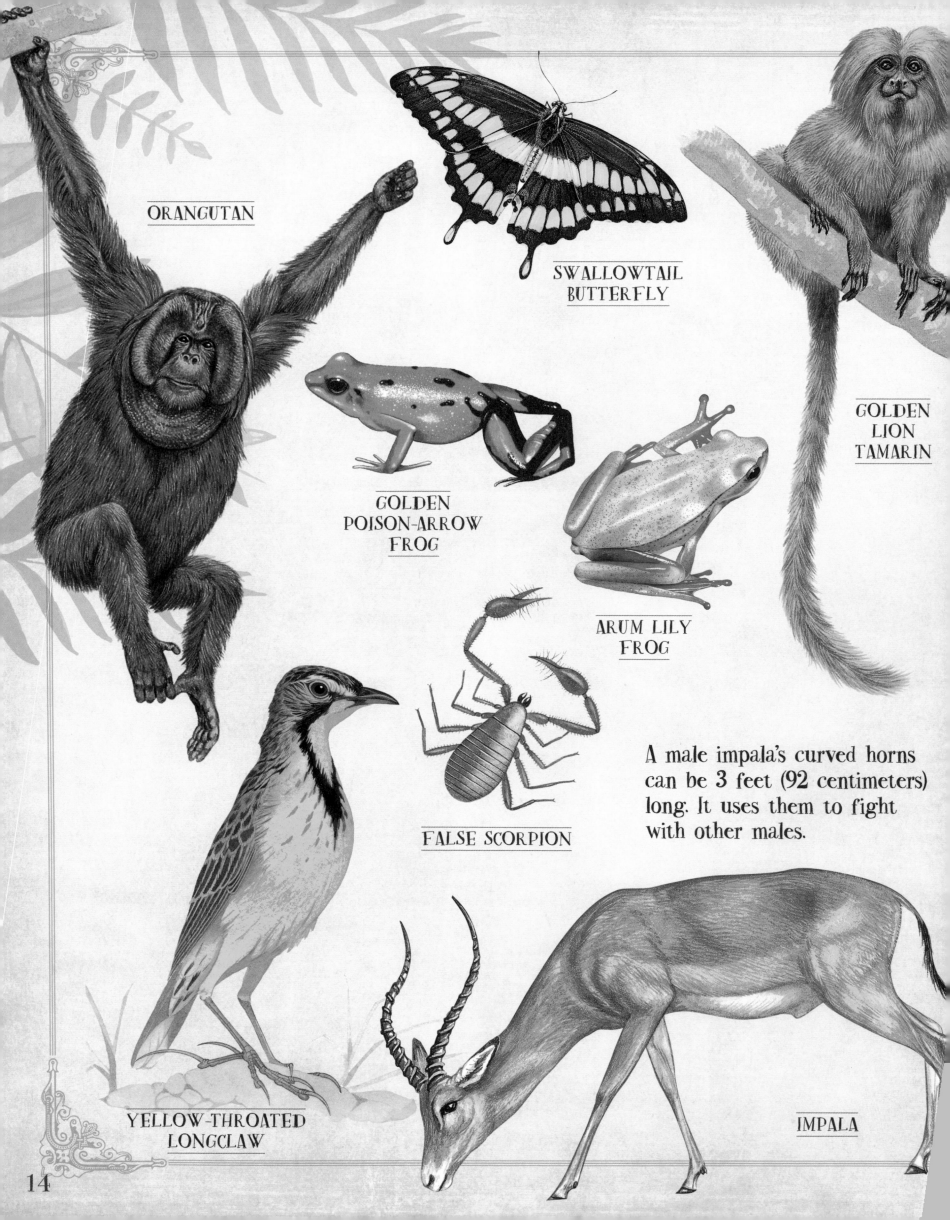

ORANGUTAN

SWALLOWTAIL
BUTTERFLY

GOLDEN
LION
TAMARIN

GOLDEN
POISON-ARROW
FROG

ARUM LILY
FROG

A male impala's curved horns
can be 3 feet (92 centimeters)
long. It uses them to fight
with other males.

FALSE SCORPION

YELLOW-THROATED
LONGCLAW

IMPALA

14

The greater fruit bat has the largest wingspan of any bat: up to 5 feet (1.5 meters) across.

GOLDEN MOUSE

GREATER FRUIT BAT

The Sunny Side of Life

Shades of orange, yellow, and gold make these animals shine like a beautiful sunrise.

CLICK BEETLE

METALMARK BUTTERFLY

GOLDEN ORIOLE

PLANT BUG

PANAMANIAN GOLD FROG

Only male lions have thick manes.

ATLAS MOTH

LIONS

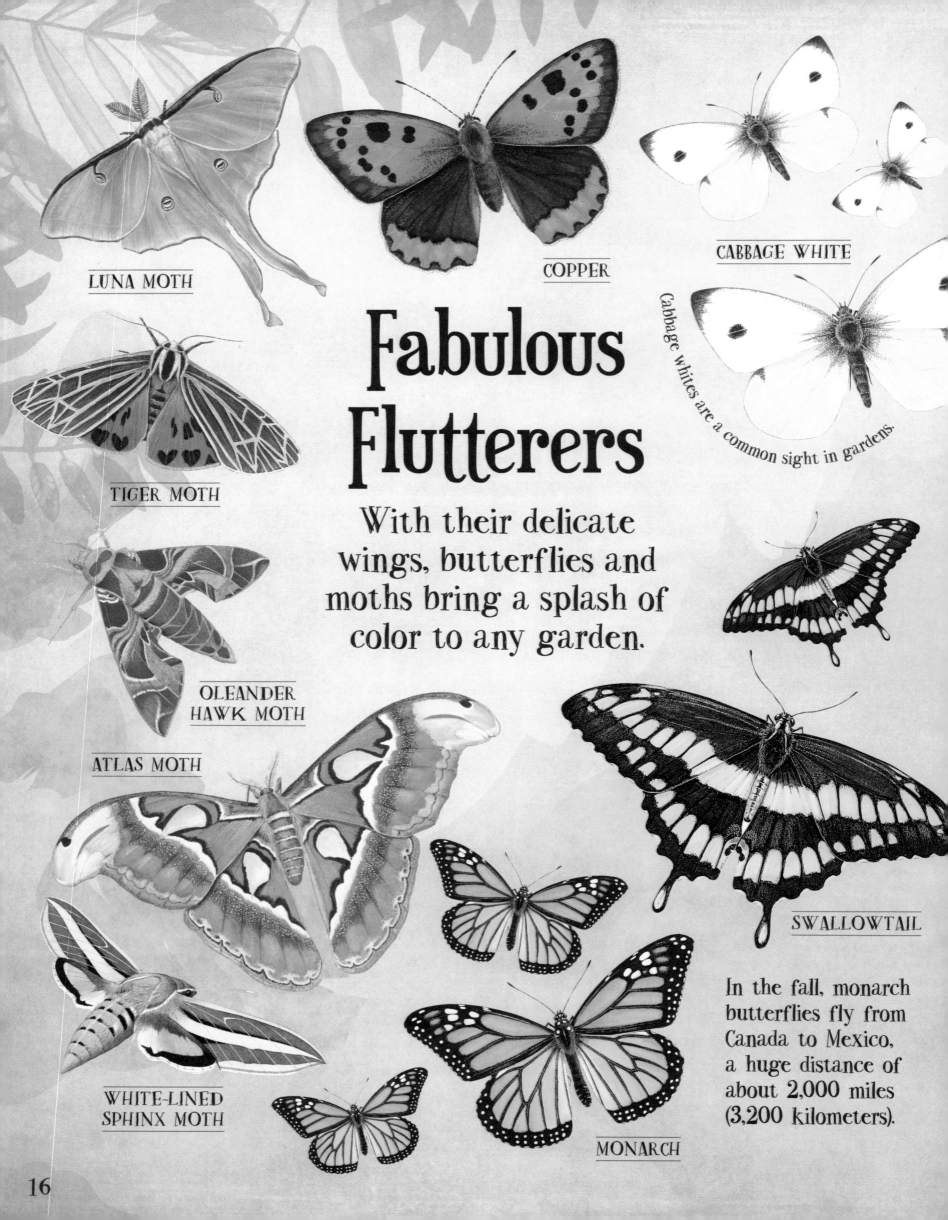

LUNA MOTH

COPPER

CABBAGE WHITE

Cabbage whites are a common sight in gardens.

Fabulous Flutterers

With their delicate wings, butterflies and moths bring a splash of color to any garden.

TIGER MOTH

OLEANDER HAWK MOTH

ATLAS MOTH

SWALLOWTAIL

WHITE-LINED SPHINX MOTH

MONARCH

In the fall, monarch butterflies fly from Canada to Mexico, a huge distance of about 2,000 miles (3,200 kilometers).

GEOMETRID
MOTH

CAIRNS
BIRDWING

POPLAR SPHINX
MOTH

Birdwing butterflies live in Asia and Australia.

The Queen Alexandra's birdwing is the world's biggest butterfly, with a wingspan of 11 inches (28 centimeters).

MORPHO

COTTON
BOLL MOTH

QUEEN ALEXANDRA'S
BIRDWING

FLUMINENSE
SWALLOWTAIL

BEE SPHINX MOTH

FENNEC FOX

GREAT JERBOA

KOALA

DEER MOUSE

CHINCHILLA

Some of these "ears"
are not ears at all.
Which of these animals
is faking it?

ANSWER ON PAGE 64

RABBIT

A rabbit can swivel its
long ears in different
directions to listen for
the sound of predators.

LONG-EARED
OWL

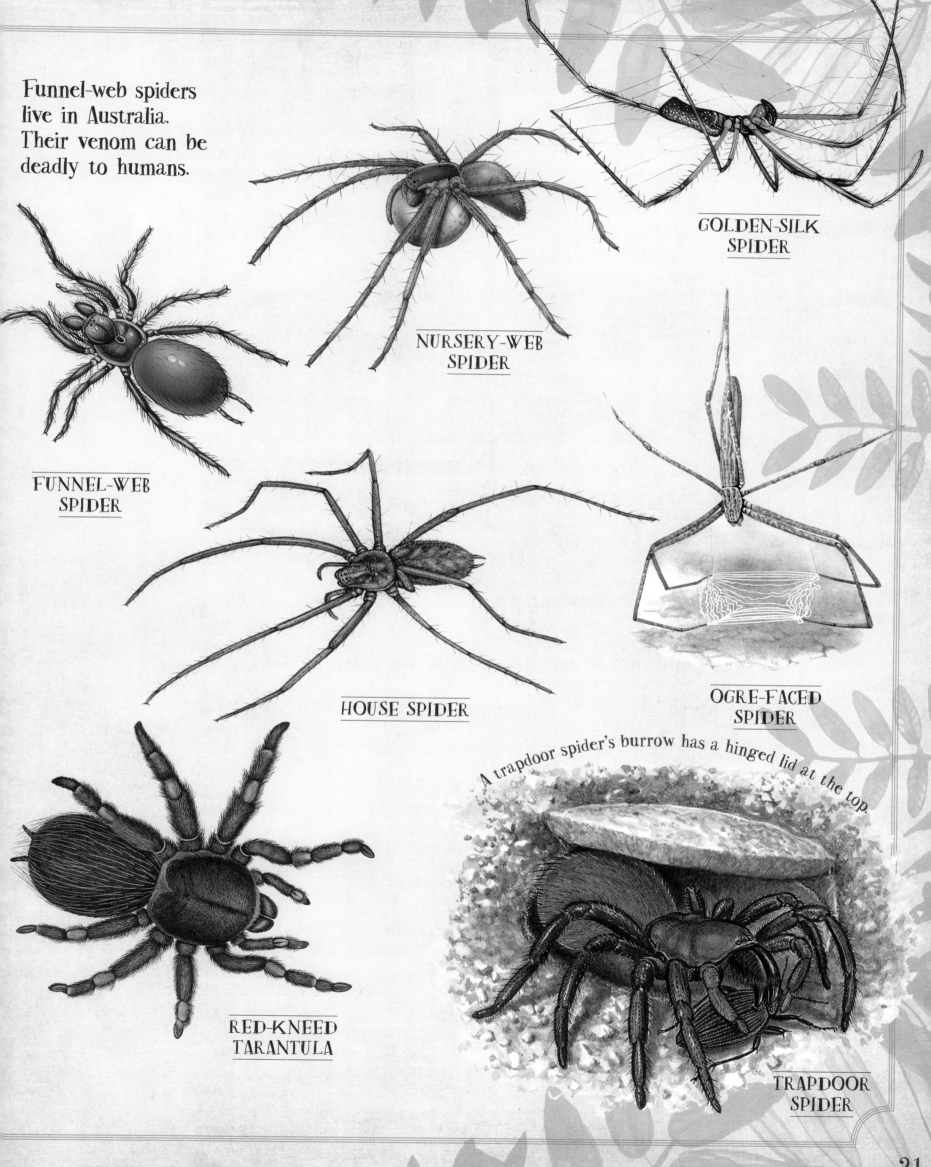

Funnel-web spiders live in Australia. Their venom can be deadly to humans.

GOLDEN-SILK SPIDER

NURSERY-WEB SPIDER

FUNNEL-WEB SPIDER

HOUSE SPIDER

OGRE-FACED SPIDER

A trapdoor spider's burrow has a hinged lid at the top.

RED-KNEED TARANTULA

TRAPDOOR SPIDER

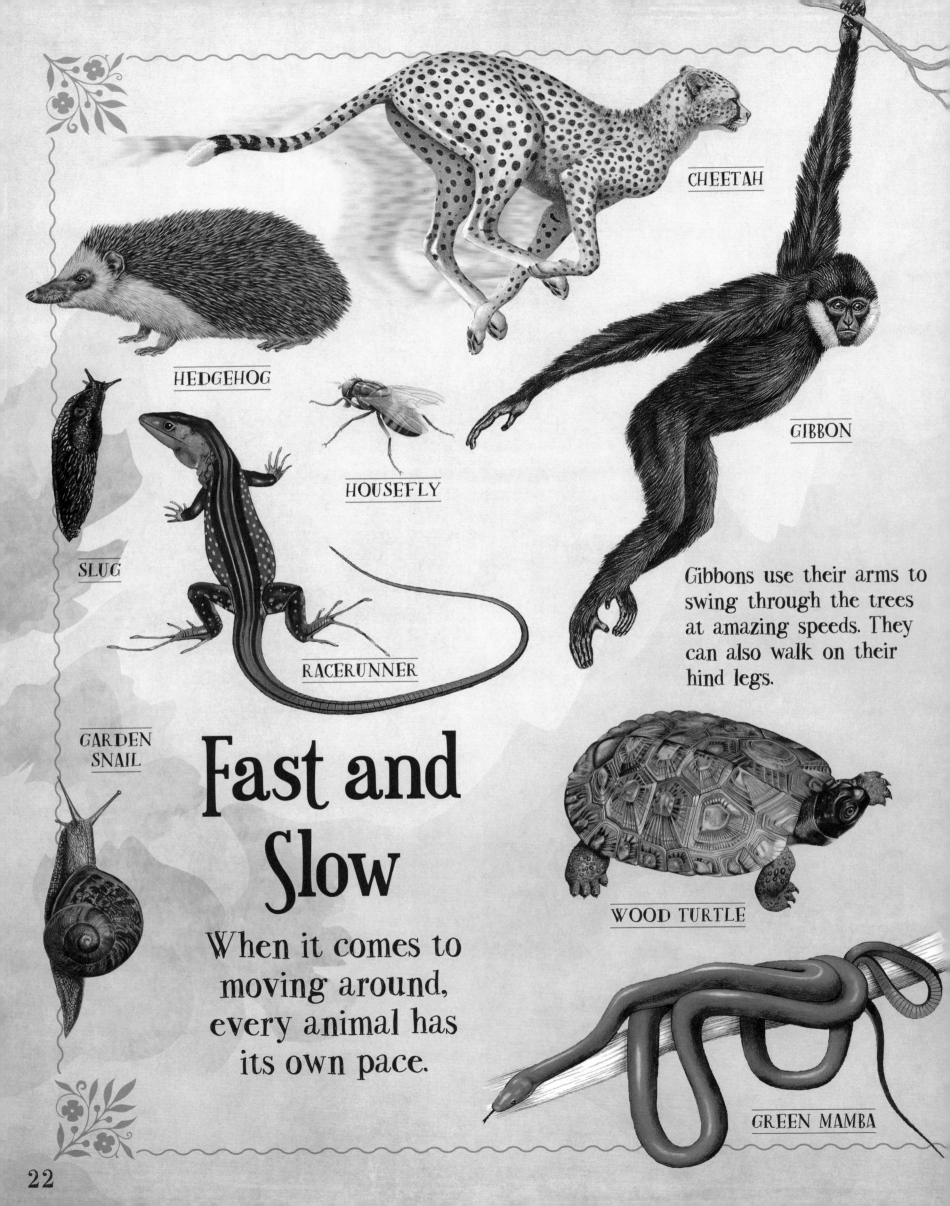

CHEETAH

HEDGEHOG

GIBBON

HOUSEFLY

SLUG

RACERUNNER

Gibbons use their arms to swing through the trees at amazing speeds. They can also walk on their hind legs.

GARDEN SNAIL

Fast and Slow

When it comes to moving around, every animal has its own pace.

WOOD TURTLE

GREEN MAMBA

CATERPILLAR

THREE-TOED SLOTH

GRASSHOPPER

RED-KNEED TARANTULA

A sloth moves incredibly slowly through the trees. It can even sleep while hanging from a branch!

ROADRUNNER

FLEA

Rheas are too heavy to fly, but they can run fast.

If these animals had a race, which do you think would win?

ANSWER ON PAGE 64

MIDGE

GREATER RHEA

23

ELEPHANT

EARWIG

RED DEER

STAG BEETLE

PORCUPINE

COMMON IGUANA

Although rhinos are big and heavy, they can run at speeds of up to 30 miles (48 kilometres) per hour.

RHINOCEROS

Caribou migrate huge distances across the Arctic tundra to look for food. Both males and females have antlers.

Only male Hercules beetles have horns.

HERCULES BEETLE

Spikes and Horns

These horns and spikes can be incredibly useful—and they look cool, too!

CARIBOU

JACKSON'S CHAMELEON

The thick coat of a musk ox keeps it warm in cold habitats.

TREEHOPPER

TUATARA

MUSK OX

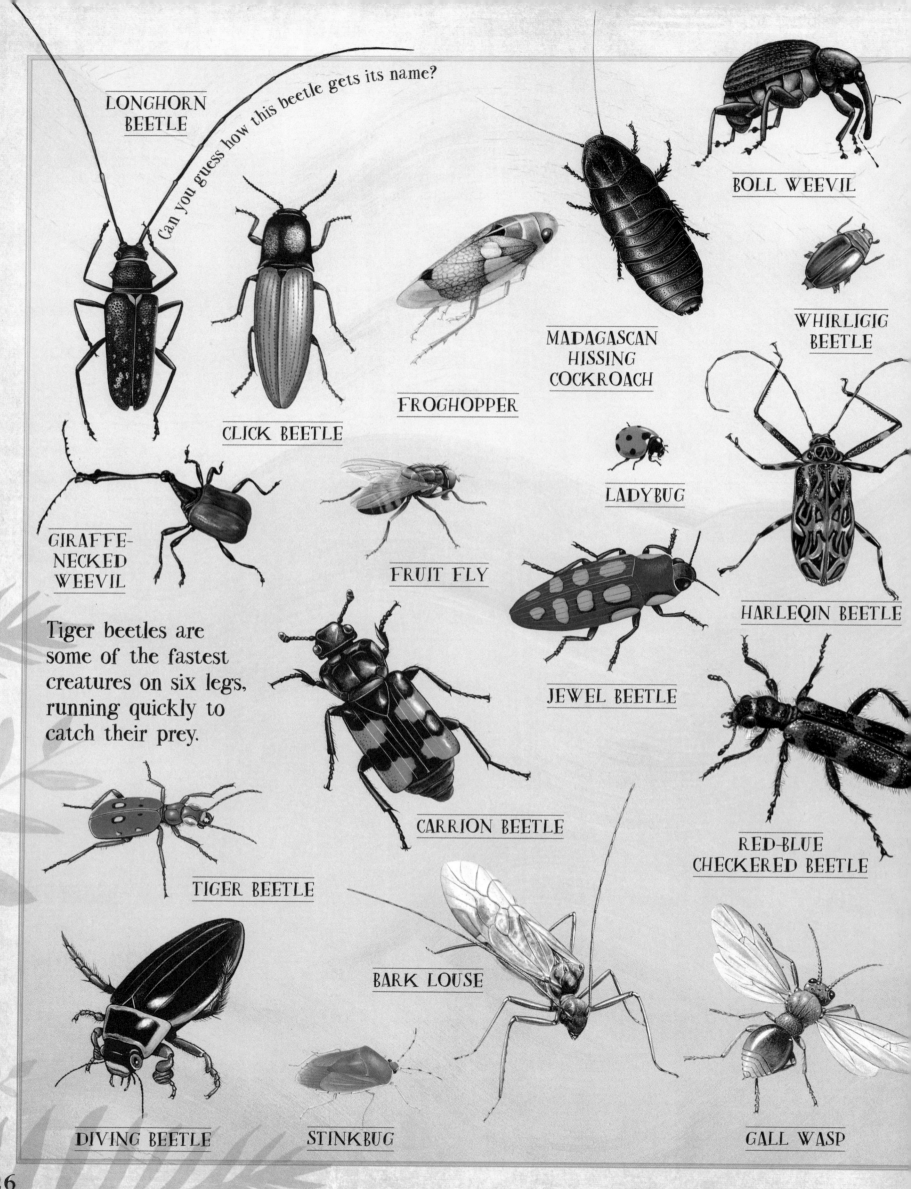

LONGHORN BEETLE

Can you guess how this beetle gets its name?

BOLL WEEVIL

CLICK BEETLE

FROGHOPPER

MADAGASCAN HISSING COCKROACH

WHIRLIGIG BEETLE

GIRAFFE-NECKED WEEVIL

FRUIT FLY

LADYBUG

HARLEQIN BEETLE

Tiger beetles are some of the fastest creatures on six legs, running quickly to catch their prey.

JEWEL BEETLE

CARRION BEETLE

RED-BLUE CHECKERED BEETLE

TIGER BEETLE

DIVING BEETLE

BARK LOUSE

STINKBUG

GALL WASP

HOVER FLY

Darkling beetles hide under stones, then scurry out at night to find food such as rotten wood and insect larvae.

GOLIATH BEETLE

CRANE FLY

BEDBUG

DUNG BEETLE

Incredible Insects

STAG BEETLE

DARKLING BEETLE

MIDGE

Marching on six legs, beetles and other insects can be found in every corner of the world.

ROBBER FLY

TEN-LINED JUNE BEETLE

PLANT BUG

CATERPILLAR HUNTER

CHIGOE FLEA

NARROW-WINGED DAMSELFLY

ROVE BEETLE

HARVESTER ANT

27

Beautiful Birds

With their fabulous feathers, birds really know how to impress.

RIBBON-TAILED ASTRABIA

BLUE BIRD-OF-PARADISE

Lyrebirds can imitate sounds such as car alarms and chainsaws!

RED-TUFTED MALACHITE SUNBIRD

The head plumes on a male King of Saxony bird are twice as long as his body. He can make them stand straight up!

KING OF SAXONY BIRD

SUPERB LYREBIRD

CRIMSON TOPAZ

RAGGIANA BIRD-OF-PARADISE

RUBY-THROATED HUMMINGBIRD

When females are near, a group of male Raggianas will hop around, flapping their wings and making high-pitched calls.

MARVELLOUS SPATULETAIL

WILSON'S BIRD-OF-PARADISE

QUETZAL

ROYAL FLYCATCHER

WIRE-TAILED MANAKIN

WILD CAT

WARTHOG

KOMODO DRAGON

This gopher has cheek pouches for storing food.

PLAINS POCKET GOPHER

Chinese water deer don't have antlers, but the males have long tusks for fighting off predators.

CASSOWARY

CHINESE WATER DEER

GIANT MOLE RAT

BABIRUSA

OSPREY

Teeth, Tusks, and Claws

Sharp claws, slashing teeth, and terrible tusks make these animals a force to be reckoned with.

BIG-EARED BAT

Bald eagles have four long, sharp talons on each foot. One of the rear talons is longer than the others.

BALD EAGLE

EUROPEAN MOLE

GRAY WOLF

KIWI

TOUCAN

Amazing Beaks

The shape of a bird's beak depends on what it eats. Can you guess which foods any of these birds likes best?

HUMMINGBIRD

RAINBOW LORIKEET

Wild turkeys can fly for short distances, but most of the time they walk along the ground, looking for seeds, nuts, insects, and lizards.

PUFFIN

TURKEY

SPARROW

FLAMINGO

This bird is the ancestor of dometic chickens.

RED JUNGLEFOWL

AVOCET

The oystercatcher's long beak is strong enough to pull shellfish off rocks and to pry open their hard shells.

PEREGRINE FALCON

OYSTERCATCHER

BROWN PELICAN

GROUND HORNBILL

EIDER DUCK

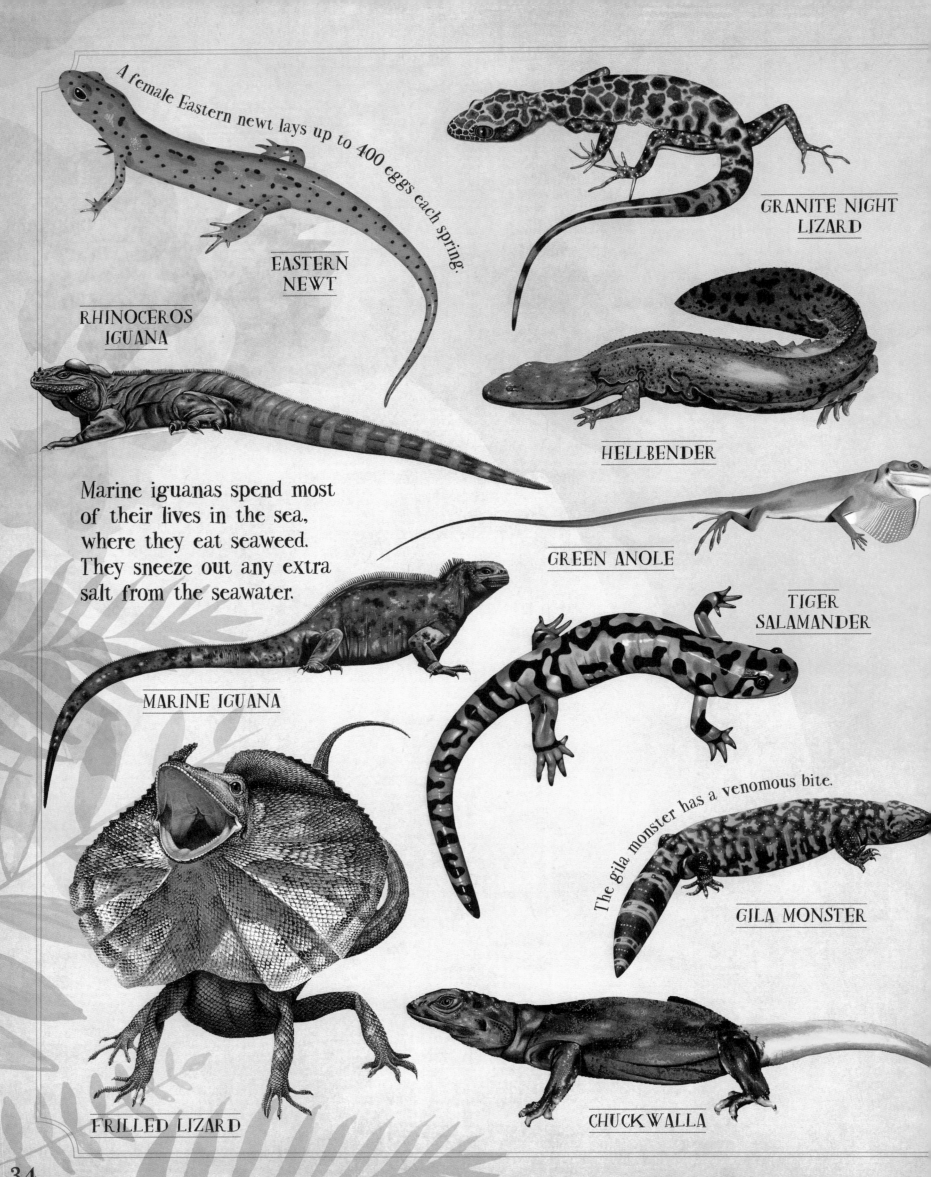

A female Eastern newt lays up to 400 eggs each spring.

GRANITE NIGHT LIZARD

EASTERN NEWT

RHINOCEROS IGUANA

HELLBENDER

Marine iguanas spend most of their lives in the sea, where they eat seaweed. They sneeze out any extra salt from the seawater.

GREEN ANOLE

TIGER SALAMANDER

MARINE IGUANA

The gila monster has a venomous bite.

GILA MONSTER

FRILLED LIZARD

CHUCKWALLA

Spotted salamanders are usually black, but they can also be blue, dark green, or dark brown.

SPOTTED SALAMANDER

KOMODO DRAGON

COMMON IGUANA

Lizards and Salamanders

Lizards are scaly and salamanders are slimy, but they both have four legs and a tail.

RED SALAMANDER

TUATARA

GREAT PLAINS SKINK

CENTRALIAN BLUE-TONGUED SKINK

FIRE SALAMANDER

GROUND LIZARD

PACIFIC GIANT SALAMANDER

ANT

The fierce grizzly bear is a type of brown bear.

BROWN BEAR

HIPPOPOTAMUS

GIRAFFE

HUMMINGBIRD

WREN

The killer whale is actually the largest type of dolphin in the world. It can be 32 feet (9.7 meters) long.

SILVERFISH

CATERPILLAR

"Hippopotamus" means "river horse" in Greek. They stay cool in rivers and graze on the grassy banks.

BEDBUG

Big and Small

From tiny insects to enormous elephants, animals come in all sizes.

MOUSE

ELEPHANT

KILLER WHALE

OSTRICH

37

Splendid Stripes

Stripes can help an animal blend in with the background, or stand out from the crowd.

CORROBOREE FROG

PLANT BUG

PRAIRIE CHICKEN

SWALLOWTAIL
BUTTERFLY

STREAKED TENREC

BEE

TIGER

A tiger's stripes help it to hide in long grasses as it sneaks up on prey such as wild pigs, buffalo, and deer.

BONGO

Each species of zebra has a different pattern of stripes.

ZEBRA

RED PANDA

Red pandas are slightly larger than domestic cats. They lick their front paws and use them to clean their faces, just like cats!

Ring-tailed lemurs live only on the island of Madagascar.

BLUE-TONGUED SKINK

INDIAN PALM SQUIRREL

RING-TAILED LEMUR

PACA

WILD BOAR

INDIAN
ELEPHANT

Elephant shrews can hop like kangaroos.

ELEPHANT
SHREW

Nifty Noses

Each of these animals "nose" how to sniff out danger–or dinner!

MANDRILL

TAPIR

Mandrills are the largest type of monkey in the world. They live in the humid rain forests of central Africa.

The male proboscis monkey's nose can act like a loudspeaker, letting him warn other monkeys of danger.

GAVIAL

PROBOSCIS MONKEY

Echidnas are mammals, but they lay eggs!

AARDVARK

ECHIDNA

What can use its nose to carry water, pick things up, and stroke its baby?

ANSWER ON PAGE 64

DARWIN'S FROG

GIANT ANTEATER

HOG-NOSED SKUNK

Legs and Feet

Some have two and some have twenty, but these animals show how legs can come in all shapes and sizes!

NORTHERN JACANA

WATER OPOSSUM

WOODCHUCK

LONGHORN BEETLE

BLUE-BLACK SPIDER WASP

Giant tortoises can live for well over 100 years.

MILLIPEDE

GREAT JERBOA

COMMON HOUSE SPIDER

GALAPAGOS GIANT TORTOISE

ANT

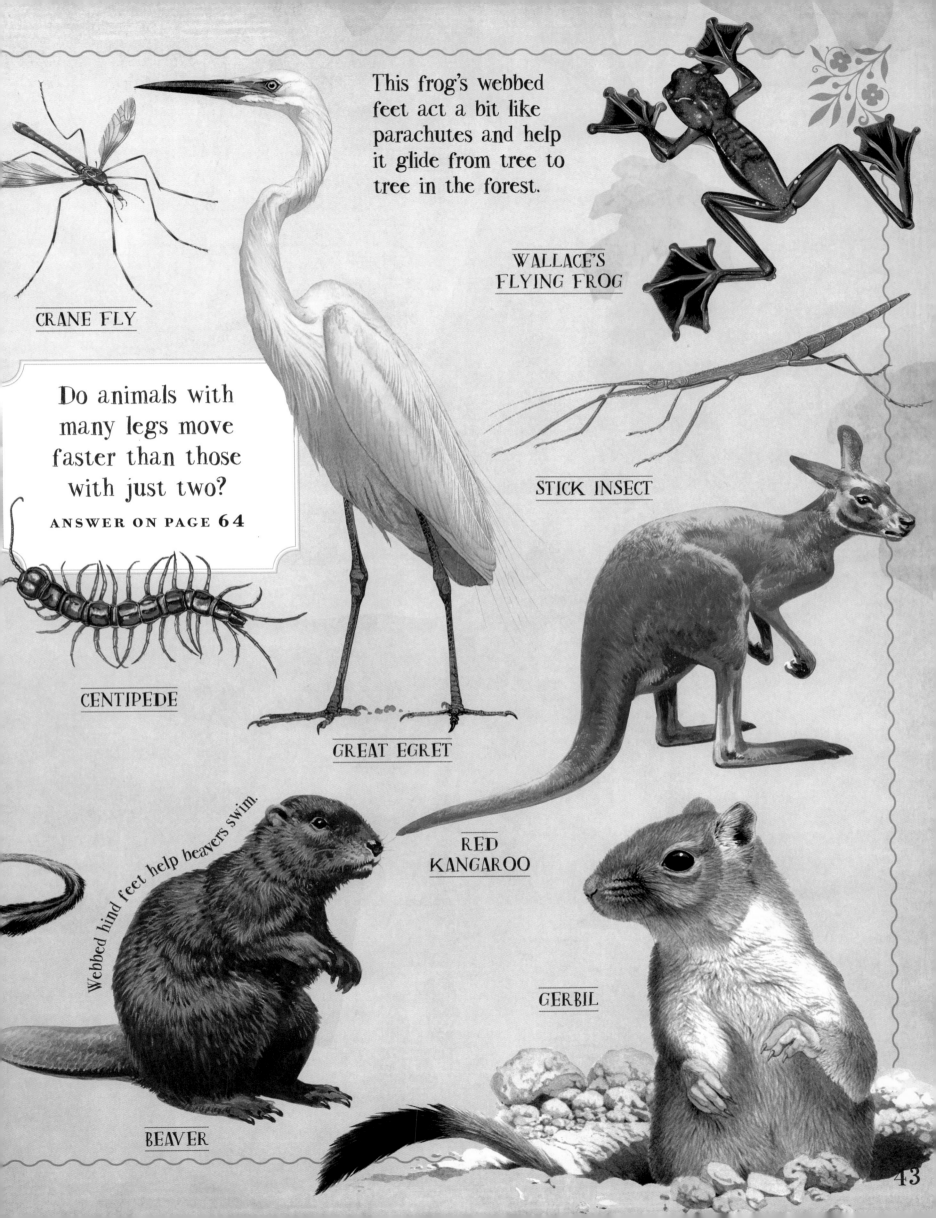

CRANE FLY

This frog's webbed feet act a bit like parachutes and help it glide from tree to tree in the forest.

WALLACE'S FLYING FROG

Do animals with many legs move faster than those with just two?

ANSWER ON PAGE 64

STICK INSECT

CENTIPEDE

GREAT EGRET

RED KANGAROO

Webbed hind feet help beavers swim.

BEAVER

GERBIL

43

PANDA

BLACK WIDOW
SPIDER

TUNDRA SWAN

It can take a giant panda up
to 15 hours a day to eat
enough bamboo to survive.

GREATER SIREN
SALAMANDER

EURASIAN
BADGER

Adult male gorillas have silvery hair on their backs.

TORRENT
TYRANNULET

GORILLA

GOLIATH
BEETLE

POLAR BEAR

SNOW BUNTING

ROVE BEETLE

ARABIAN ORYX

Black and White

It's a colorful world, but not for these creatures. They're elegant in monochrome.

ARCTIC HARE

GREAT BLACK SLUG

SKUNK

When threatened by a predator, a skunk sprays terrible-smelling liquid from glands near its tail.

AMERICAN CROW

ARCTIC FOX

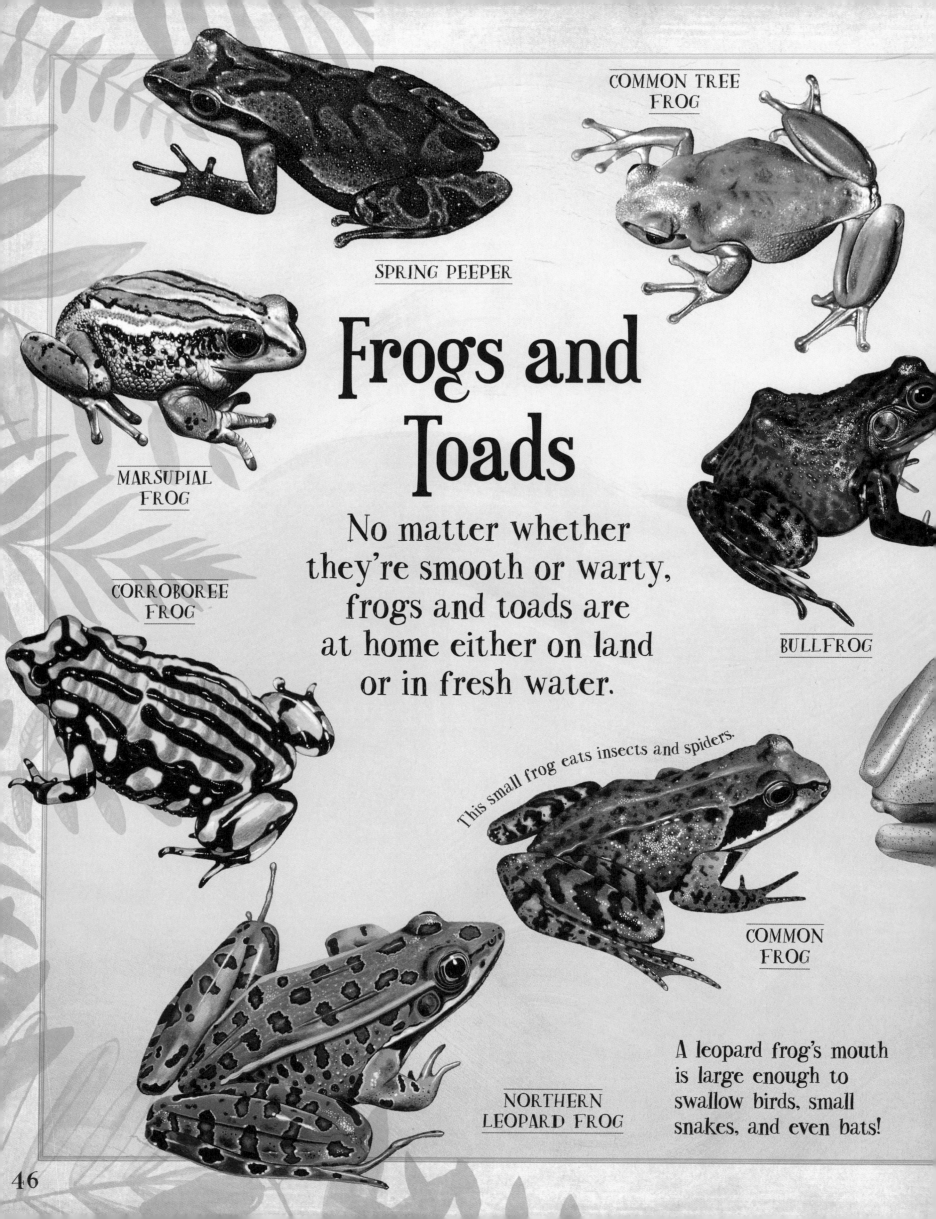

COMMON TREE
FROG

SPRING PEEPER

Frogs and Toads

No matter whether
they're smooth or warty,
frogs and toads are
at home either on land
or in fresh water.

MARSUPIAL
FROG

CORROBOREE
FROG

BULLFROG

This small frog eats insects and spiders.

COMMON
FROG

NORTHERN
LEOPARD FROG

A leopard frog's mouth
is large enough to
swallow birds, small
snakes, and even bats!

ORIENTAL FIRE-
BELLIED TOAD

NARROW-
MOUTHED TOAD

MARSH TOAD

This large frog will eat anything it can catch.

WESTERN SPADEFOOT

DARWIN'S
FROG

ARUM LILY
FROG

AMAZON
HORNED FROG

Natterjack toads are
loud! A male's call can
be heard up to 1.25 miles
(2 kilometers) away.

NATAL GHOST
FROG

NATTERJACK TOAD

Leaf-tailed geckos cling to tree trunks, where their spotted skin helps them blend in with the bark.

FLAP-NECKED CHAMELEON

LEAF-TAILED GECKO

GABOON VIPER

The venomous Gaboon viper has a deadly bite.

MATAMATA

BROWN BANDICOOT

GREY POTOO

FLOWER MANTIS

GRASS SNAKE

ooking like a stick protects this insect from birds.

STICK INSECT

SLENDER
LORIS

Hide and
Seek

You'll have to look
very carefully to spot
these masters of
camouflage in the wild.

GREAT TINAMOU

PANCAKE
TORTOISE

POORWILL

Unlike other birds, the
poorwill hibernates in
winter. It hides in piles
of rocks to rest and wait
for warmer weather.

ANGOLA
MANTIS

LONG-HORNED
GRASSHOPPER

KATYDID

SEA LILY

TREE PANGOLIN

SOUTH AFRICAN RAIN FROG

ROBBER FLY

Weird and Wonderful

Some animals are completely unique. These creatures could never be mistaken for another!

A chameleon's long tongue has a sticky pad at the tip. It can shoot it out quickly to catch passing insects.

WARTY NEWT

CHAMELEON

HERMIT IBIS

Naked mole-rats live in giant underground colonies.

NAKED MOLE-RAT

GLASS FROG

VELVET ANT

INDRI

Which of these animals carries its babies in an unusual way?

ANSWER ON PAGE 64

GIANT ARMADILLO

Giant armadillos use their large front claws to rip into termite mounds, and dig for worms and other prey.

CORROBOREE FROG

MOLE CRICKET

CROCODILE

SUN BITTERN

GREATER GLIDER

EARWIG

The greater glider comes out of its den at night to eat the leaves and buds of eucalyptus trees.

BROWN LONG-EARED BAT

MIDGE

WARBLER

Even with these amazing wings, ostriches are still too heavy to fly.

OSTRICH

HUMMINGBIRD MOTH

BIDDY

STORM PETREL

COMMON TERN

Fabulous Wings

These amazing wings help birds and insects move as they run or fly.

GULL

A red kite uses its wings to soar through the air as it searches for birds, reptiles, rats, or carrion.

RED KITE

QUEEN ALEXANDRA'S BIRDWING

What appears to fly but doesn't have wings?

ANSWER ON PAGE 64

ANTLION

KING VULTURE

BOA CONSTRICTOR

ASSASSIN BUG

Assassin bugs use their saliva to paralyze their prey before eating it.

OLIVE BABOON

EURASIAN LYNX

Chimpanzees work in groups to hunt monkeys.

CHIMPANZEE

LION

BUSH DOG

54

SPEAR-NOSED
BAT

GOLDEN
EAGLE

PARADISE
TREE SNAKE

Ferocious Hunters

No animal is safe from
these master predators.

FIRE
ANT

RED-TAILED
HAWK

TRANSVAAL
SNAKE LIZARD

TIGER
BEETLE

A mongoose isn't
afraid to take on
dangerous prey such
as a cobra. The
snake's venom doesn't
hurt it.

This bird hunts small mammals such as lemmings and voles.

MONGOOSE

ROUGH-LEGGED
BUZZARD

RED-TAILED TROPIC BIRD

EMPEROR TAMARIN

LYRE-TAILED NIGHTJAR

SCORPION

Tremendous Tails

Whether they're for balance, grabbing, or simply looking great, these tails make a real impact.

Kowaris live in the deserts and grasslands of Australia.

KOWARI

Which of these creatures has a stinger?

ANSWER ON PAGE 64

CLUBTAIL DRAGONFLY

The zorilla lives in Africa and although it looks a bit like a skunk, it is actually a type of weasel.

ZORILLA

This jacamar perches on a tree branch, waiting for insects to fly by, then darts out to catch them in its beak.

MELLER'S CHAMELEON

RUFOUS-TAILED JACAMAR

MACAW

LUMHOLTZ'S TREE KANGAROO

MAYFLY

RED SQUIRREL

DESERT KANGAROO RAT

FIREFLY

WOOD MOUSE

Hutias shelter in their burrows during the day.

BARN OWL

BAHAMIAN HUTIA

Binturongs live in the forests of Southeast Asia, and they are sometimes called "bearcats." Can you guess why?

BROWN KIWI

BINTURONG

GRANITE
LIZARD

GREATER FALSE
VAMPIRE BAT

DESERT
DORMOUSE

CALIFORNIA SLENDER
SALAMANDER

Night Owls

Some animals love
the nightlife! These
creatures come out
when it's dark.

False vampire bats do
not drink blood. They
come out at night to
catch insects, rodents,
frogs, and fish.

NIGHTJAR

CARACAL

KINKAJOU

COTTON BOLL
MOTH

GOOSE BARNACLE

GHOST BAT

Firebrats like to live where it is warm, and they often make their homes indoors, near ovens or furnaces.

FIREBRAT

Incredibly Hairy

FUNNEL-WEB SPIDER

Hair and fur can provide camouflage, help keep an animal warm, or make it look fabulous.

VIRGINIA OPOSSUM

The maned wolf looks like a fox, but with really long legs.

AARDWOLF

MANED WOLF

MONK SAKI

CARPENTER BEE

WHITE-LINED SPHINX MOTH

JAPANESE MACAQUE

Each spectacled bear has a slightly different pattern of markings on its face, which helps scientists tell them apart.

This is the smallest and hairiest type of rhinoceros.

SUMATRAN RHINO

SPECTACLED BEAR

Only mammals have real fur. How many of these animals are faking it?

ANSWER ON PAGE 64

WIND SCORPION

Hot and Cold

These animals are able to live in some of the most extreme environments on Earth.

ARCTIC HARE

A polar bear's hollow hairs help keep it insulated.

NORWAY LEMMING

SNOWY SHEATHBILL

POLAR BEAR

In the winter, a moose uses its hooves to shovel away the snow to find moss and lichen to eat.

MOOSE

GERBOA

SECRETARY
BIRD

GREEN IGUANA

MEERKAT

INDIAN
PYTHON

A camel's hump stores fat, which it can break down into water and energy.

Gila monsters are one of only a few types of venomous lizards. They live in the deserts of the southwestern United States.

CAMEL

GILA MONSTER

Answers

INTERESTING EYES

Q: Most animals have two eyes. Which of these creatures has more than two?

A: Most animals have two eyes. The wolf spider has eight.

SUPER SCARY

Q: Which of these super scary animals is the strongest, for its size?

A: The stag beetle is incredibly strong for its size, making it one of the world's strongest beasts.

WEIRD EARS

Q: Some of these "ears" are not ears at all. Which of these animals is faking it?

A: The long-eared owl's ear tufts aren't ears at all–they just make it look bigger and scarier.

FAST AND SLOW

Q: If these animals had a race, which do you think would win?

A: The cheetah would win. It can reach a top speed of more than 60 miles (97 kilometers) per hour.

NIFTY NOSES

Q: What can use its nose to carry water, pick things up, and stroke its baby?

A: The elephant: its nose is called a trunk; it is really strong and very useful.

LEGS AND FEET

Q: Do animals with many legs move faster than those with just two?

A: Four legs are faster than two, but for its size, the spider, ant, and centipede can move very fast with more!

WEIRD AND WONDERFUL

Q: Which of these animals carries its babies in an unusual way?

A: The crocodile carries its young in an unusual way. It holds them in its mouth!

FABULOUS WINGS

Q: What appears to fly but doesn't have wings?

A: The glider's skin helps it glide, but it doesn't have wings to fly.

TREMENDOUS TAILS

Q: Which of these creatures has a stinger?

A: The scorpion protects itself from predators by using its tail to sting.

INCREDIBLY HAIRY

Q: Only mammals have real fur. How many of these animals are faking it?

A: Six animals are faking it: the barnacle, spider, firebrat, moth, bee and wind scorpion.